Business Alignment
STRATEGIES, INC.

2511 Belmont Avenue
Long Beach, CA 90815
www.BusinessAlignmentStrategies.com

© 2013 by Pat Lynch. All rights reserved.

This publication contains the opinions and ideas of its author and is designed to provide useful advice to the reader on the subject matter covered. The author specifically disclaims any responsibility for any liability, loss, or risk that may be claimed or incurred as a consequence, directly or indirectly, of the use and/or application of any of the contents of this publication.

Send feedback to Info@BusinessAlignmentStrategies.com

Printed in the United States of America

ISBN: 978-0-9827324-3-4

Art Direction & Layout by:
Peter A. Colón
YourGoToGirls.com

Survey Says...:
The Professionals' Guide To Great Surveys

Pat Lynch, Ph.D.

Acknowledgement

The groundwork for my expertise in survey development, administration, analysis, and reporting was laid during my doctoral program at the Beebe Institute of Personnel and Employment Relations in the College of Business Administration at Georgia State University. I would like to recognize four of my professors whose efforts ensured that foundation was a solid and long-lasting one.

My first assignment as a brand new doctoral student who knew nothing about surveys or academic research was to work with Dr. Sandy Wayne as a research assistant. No doubt her heart sank when my answer to a question about how to interpret survey results revealed that I had no clue what they meant. I thank Sandy for introducing me to survey research, and for her patience and perseverance in teaching me the basics.

I am grateful to Dr. Paul Swiercz, who helped me develop my first survey-based research project. Paul's guidance not only resulted in a successful outcome, but helped me realize that survey research was great fun!

Dr. Lynn Shore taught me one of the most important lessons of effective survey design: if the data from a question will not help inform the purpose of the survey, don't ask the question. Because my curiosity about related but "nice to know" issues tended to lure me off on tangents, I needed someone to help keep me on the straight and narrow. I thank Lynn for being relentless in reminding me to stay focused on the purpose of the survey.

Dr. Vida Scarpello, a recognized master of survey research, taught me many of the "secrets" contained herein, and guided me as I applied them in both my doctoral dissertation and other research projects. I am forever grateful to Vida for making sure that I was well prepared to conduct effective academic and applied survey research.

In addition to my consulting clients for whom I have conducted employee or customer surveys over the years, I also would like to thank the many students I worked with on various applied research projects during my academic career, and the organizations that allowed us access to their workforces. Applying my survey skills in "real life" situations and teaching those skills to others have allowed me to help improve others' conditions – and to have fun!

Finally, I would be remiss if I did not thank the HR Certification Institute (HRCI) for the training it provided me when I signed on as a volunteer item writer for the national PHR and SPHR exams in 2001. Despite my rigorous academic training and extensive applied experience in developing surveys, the HRCI training raised my item writing skills to a whole new level.

Table of Contents

Introduction

Tired of spending countless hours creating and conducting customer surveys only to find you can't do anything with the results? Are you frustrated by all the time and money you've wasted on research and development while gaining little to no usable information from surveying your employees? You need professional advice on how to develop and administer reliable, results-driven surveys that obtain accurate, actionable information from your employees and customers. You have come to the right place.

In this booklet you will learn Insider Secrets from survey experts on every aspect of developing, designing, conducting and analyzing surveys, with a final section devoted to the ultimate goal and purpose of a survey: Reporting Results and Taking Action.

Survey Says... The Professionals' Guide To Great Surveys is a practical guide for anyone who has the responsibility for conducting workplace (employee) or business (customer) surveys. It will walk you step-by-step through all five stages of the survey process: planning, designing, administering, analyzing, and reporting results and taking action. Each chapter contains an INSIDER TIP that will maximize the effectiveness of your survey process.

Inside you'll discover how to:

- Manage critical success factors
- Assess a survey expert's fit for your needs
- Write effective survey questions
- Choose an online vendor
- Maximize your response rate
- Report accurate and comprehensive results
- Avoid overlooking the one most critical step of every survey process

Learn valuable, time-tested tips and techniques rarely discussed outside of select graduate level academic programs. Benefit from my decades of education and hands-on experience in designing, implementing and evaluating workplace surveys. In this booklet, I have revealed the Insider Secrets you need to create and conduct the optimal survey to get the results you need to take action to improve your business.

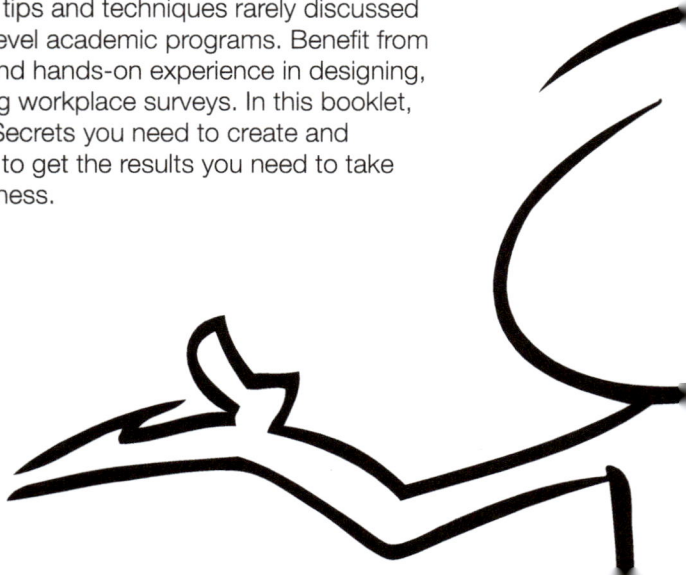

From my days as a doctoral student and throughout my career as a survey professional, I have reviewed hundreds upon hundreds of customer and employee surveys over the years. Their widespread ineffectiveness, the unnecessary waste of time and effort, and the lack of clear, easy-to-follow practical resources motivated me to compile this booklet of Insider Secrets to benefit everyone who is interested in conducting accurate, comprehensive and actionable surveys in their workplace. Although careful planning and attention to detail are time consuming, the payback in terms of accurate information far outweighs your investment. Using my step-by-step process and the Insider Secrets you learn in this booklet, you can ensure your survey results are valid, complete, and as useful as possible.

Insider Secret #1:
The quality of preparation during the planning and design stages is key to a successful survey process. By picking up this booklet, you are already on your way to creating and developing your most successful survey ever. Learn information that you will find in no other comprehensive resources on surveys. The survey development process you will learn will greatly increase the quality of your data and the effectiveness of the actions you take based on them.

Insider Secret #2:
Developing and administering surveys is a process, not an event. There are twenty-four chapters in this booklet, each with a relevant Insider Tip selected to help increase the quality and strength of your survey and your results. The emphasis is on the "how to" because that's where the effectiveness of the survey is achieved.

I wish you the very best in applying these Insider Secrets to drive your survey and ultimately, your organization's success. Let's get started!

Planning the Survey Process

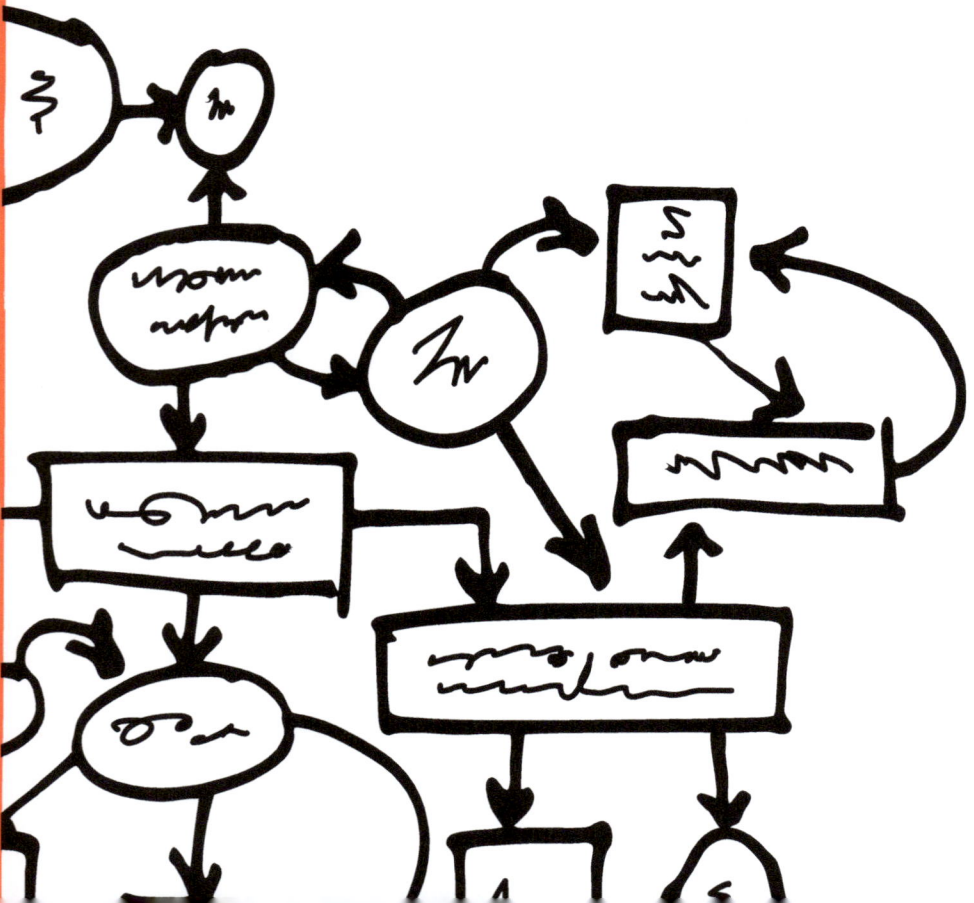

Chapter I: Critical Success Factors

Insider Tip: In the absence of critical success factors, the survey process will fail.

In order to achieve useful results from a survey process – i.e., those that are accurate and actionable – certain critical success factors must be present. Without these factors, the endeavor will fail miserably at one or more levels. For example, the results will be unusable or inaccurate, management will lose credibility, resources will be squandered, and/or employees will become cynical. In short, the organization will be worse off than it was before the survey.

Here are nine critical success factors for an effective survey process:

- **Management Buy-in and Active Support**
  If management is not engaged, why should respondents be? Employees or customers who hear nothing from management about the importance of a survey are likely to conclude that it's no big deal and/or not worth their time. Management must get out there and sell the benefits of the survey by their actions as well as by their words.

- **Management's Promise to Act on the Results**
  One of the biggest credibility wreckers is asking people to take the time to respond to a survey, and then ignoring the results. Conducting a survey creates expectations that something will happen. While responding doesn't necessarily mean agreeing to make all suggested changes, failing to take action is NOT an option.

  Two of the questions management must ask and answer truthfully in advance are, "What are we willing to do with the responses?" and, "What will we be able to do with the responses?" If the answer to either question is "nothing," do everyone a favor and stop right there.

- **A Well-Thought-out Plan for the Survey Process**
  A flawed survey process and/or content cannot possibly provide accurate and actionable results. The lack of proper planning results in an ineffective process just as surely as no planning at all. Good planning creates a solid foundation for success.

- **A Compelling Answer to the, "What's in it for me?" Question**
  The biggest motivator for adults to respond to surveys is enlightened self interest, or the factor known as, "What's in it for me?" The word ME is key: prospective participants must see the benefit that accrues to them personally, not to their team or their organization. With a plethora of competing demands on people's time, you have to let them know clearly why it's in their interest to respond to your survey.

- **Quality Questions**
  The quality of the survey items is critical to eliciting accurate and actionable

information. Quite simply, if the questions are not phrased in ways that enable responders to provide useful answers, you are wasting everyone's time and squandering the organization's resources and credibility.

- **Expertise of the Person Managing the Survey Process**
Whether you use someone from inside or outside the organization, here is the ruling criterion: Does this individual have the expertise necessary to oversee the survey process? Cost should not be an excuse to hire an unqualified person; the potential for ineffectiveness and harm is too great.

- **An Environment that Respondents Perceive as "Safe"**
People will not respond to surveys – or respond truthfully – if they believe they might suffer negative repercussions. **Perceptions** of harm are as real to individuals as is actual damage, so you must examine the safety of the survey process from **respondents'** points of view and address any concerns in the planning and design stages.

- **Effective, Ongoing Communication with Stakeholders and Participants**
The time to communicate with your various constituencies is before, during, and after the survey process. The communication plan and its implementation must be an integral part of the survey process, not an afterthought.

- **Fulfillment of the Promise to Take Action Based on the Survey Results**
Promising to take action is a necessary but insufficient precursor to obtaining accurate and actionable survey results. Fulfillment of the promise is also required. Quite simply, your employees' or customers' trust, as well as your credibility, is at stake. When the reaction to survey respondents' efforts is silence, you can be sure there will be negative consequences.

The above factors are characterized as "critical" for a simple reason. If they are not present, your survey process cannot be successful. However, if you have addressed them all, you are ready to move on to the next stage in planning your survey: achieving clarity.

Chapter 2: Clarify! Clarify! Clarify!

Insider Tip: Be very clear about the purpose of the survey. It drives the entire process.

Fuzzy planning will result in ineffective surveys that might fail to address key issues or leave you unable to act on the results. Reaching clarity during the planning stage is important because the decisions made will affect the design and/or administration of the survey, and will guide choices about how to present the data so they are useful to decision makers.

1. **Why are you conducting the survey? What is its purpose?**
    The answers to these questions drive the entire survey process because they help to identify the specific types of information you need to obtain. For example, do you want to gauge reactions to a new or proposed process, gather information so you can take action (e.g., offer a new product, service, or program), obtain clarification about an issue (e.g., what aspect of pay employees are dissatisfied with), or solve a problem (e.g., determine what's causing high employee turnover or low sales)?

2. **What topics will be covered - and not covered?**
    To conclude that identifying the purpose of a survey automatically leads to agreement about the specific topics to address would be presumptuous. Some decision makers try to include too many issues in a single survey. Others are not ready to learn, accept or respond to expected answers, so they omit serious issues. Still others find it hard to resist delving into topics that they find interesting, but have nothing to do with the purpose of the survey. Here are two clarifying questions that will help you discern what topics should and should not be addressed:
    *   Why is this topic important?
    *   How is it related to the survey's purpose?

    Every item must be related directly to the purpose of the survey. If a proposed topic is important but not related to the purpose, you may want to revisit the purpose and adjust it if appropriate. Otherwise, do not include that topic in the survey.

3. **How will you use the survey results?**
    You must have a general plan to address the survey results, whether they are expected or unexpected. If you have no idea what you will do with expected answers about a given issue, or if you are unwilling to do something about it (e.g., compensation), you shouldn't ask questions about it. You also need to be prepared for unexpected responses and develop a skill known by one non profit organization as, "situational agility," which is the ability to effectively address circumstances that one cannot anticipate but are likely to arise given the nature of the work. Developing situational agility in the context of a survey process could mean identifying a framework for addressing unexpected findings.

4. How will you create a safe environment?

Providing an environment in which people feel safe in responding truthfully to survey questions is a critical success factor. If there is a low level of trust between respondents and survey sponsors or management, assurances of safety take on more importance. One way to foster a sense of safety is by promising confidentiality or anonymity to respondents. Providing anonymity is very difficult to do, particularly in the workplace. However, confidentiality can be achieved by establishing the proper safeguards during the planning and administrative stages. You must disclose the level of confidentiality you intend to provide to survey respondents so they can make informed choices about whether or not to participate.

5. Is a survey the appropriate tool given the intended purpose and context?

Surveys are not always the appropriate tool for obtaining the desired information. For example, you don't want to burn out your customers or employees by surveying them too frequently. Sometimes decision makers are not ready to hear the answers or to take action based on what they learn. In these or similar situations, you would be well advised to consider alternatives to conducting a survey, such as conducting focus groups, interviewing individuals, or simply postponing the survey.

Once you have clarified the purpose of the survey, identified the topics to cover, specified how you will use the results, created a safe environment and confirmed that a survey is the appropriate tool, you are almost ready to delve into planning the survey logistics. First you need to select a survey expert.

Chapter 3: How to Select a Survey Expert

Insider Tip: Hire an expert. What you don't know about surveys can hurt you.

To be blunt, if you're not using an expert to develop and implement your survey, you're wasting everyone's time as well as squandering organizational resources and management credibility. Whether you use an in-house expert or contract out the survey process, you must have someone who knows what he/she is doing.

The fact that surveys often require a substantial commitment of resources means that there is a high cost associated with NOT doing them correctly. Consider these points: if your data are unreliable or inaccurate, your corrective actions will be misdirected. If you address the wrong issues, the original problems will remain unresolved. If your survey fails, trust levels and management credibility will plummet. To avoid these mishaps, here are two questions you need to answer when making the decision about how much time and effort to expend on identifying an expert to direct your survey process:

- What are the costs to the organization, employees, customers, and management of not getting the right survey expert for your needs?
- Can you live with those costs?

To avoid potential disasters, here are some questions that will help you assess an individual's level of expertise in survey development and implementation:

- What kind of training or education do you have in survey development?
- What kinds of surveys have you conducted in the past?
- Where do the survey questions come from?
- Are the survey questions customized or standardized?
- Describe a typical customer or employee survey project.
- Do you transfer your skills to your clients' staff?
- How do you help your clients move from results to action?
- What are typical client outcomes as a result of having used your survey services?

The return on the time and effort spent on due diligence in selecting an expert to manage your survey process cannot be underestimated.

An early decision must be made about whether to use an internal expert or an external one. If your organization seldom administers surveys, it probably would be cost effective to hire an external expert. Even when you have the requisite expertise in-house, you may want to consider the pros and cons of using in-house staff. The major advantages of using an in-house expert are cost and time. Generally there is a lower financial investment (assuming the individual performs other tasks), and you need not spend time interviewing and assessing outside experts. The disadvantages may include a lower response rate due to concern over a lack of confidentiality, and real or perceived pressure to obtain certain results.

The major advantages to hiring an external expert include the range of experience that person brings and his/her ability to recommend best practices as appropriate. There is no organizational "baggage" that may inadvertently bias the process, and there are no preconceived ideas or pressure to show specific answers. You also may request that this individual train your staff so you can begin to bring this function in-house over time. The major disadvantage is that if you skip the due diligence step, you may get someone who is inexperienced or who provides a "one-size-fits-all" approach that does not serve you well.

In short, identifying the survey expert is not the time to skimp on expertise or cost. In this situation, an unqualified person can cause damage that literally can take years to remedy or reverse.

Chapter 4: Survey Planning Logistics

Insider Tip: Don't promise something you cannot deliver; confidentiality and anonymity are two different things.

Two logistics-related aspects of the survey process have important implications for planning purposes: maintaining the integrity of the process and selecting the method by which to administer the survey.

In order to be effective, a survey process must be perceived by its stakeholders as having integrity. That is, it must be seen as reliable, fair and able to provide honest or truthful results. Here are three things you can do to create and maintain the integrity of the survey process:

1. **Anticipate and address the concerns of stakeholders at every step**
   Typical concerns include privacy, confidentiality, fairness, and follow-up actions. For example, both customers and employees are concerned about privacy and confidentiality. Individuals whose behaviors or results may be scrutinized (e.g., managers) are likely to focus on the fairness of the process and its implications. A low level of trust means you will need to do more work to prepare respondents so they will answer and be truthful. In general, people want to know whether it will be worth their time to respond to the survey, and whether their feedback truly will lead to change.

2. **Provide honest feedback**
   Communicating the results is key to the integrity of the process. While the type and level of feedback will differ – for example, employees may receive a summary of the results whereas senior management will receive a detailed analysis with specific recommendations – providing the information helps to establish or reinforce management's credibility.

3. **Use the results**
   Taking action is a critical success factor, as administering a survey creates expectations that something will happen. Failing to take action destroys the integrity of the process and causes management's credibility to plummet. Respondents legitimately wonder why they bothered to take the survey, and will resolve to not do so in the future.

Selecting an appropriate survey method is the second major logistical issue in the planning stage. There are two primary methods of survey administration: paper and pencil, and online. Both methods require advance planning. To determine which type best suits your purposes, consider factors that influence response rates such as privacy and confidentiality concerns, respondents' comfort level with the method, ease of use (for you and your respondents), time, and cost. Here is a brief discussion of three options for survey administration: written, face-to-face, and telephone.

1. Written Survey

   Whether administered online or by paper and pencil, the written format is the most common of the three survey methods. It is the least costly as it usually consists primarily or entirely of close-ended responses. A written survey also allows for a number of ways to provide confidentiality to respondents.

2. Face-to-Face Interviews

   Face-to-face interviews can be conducted individually or in groupings like focus groups. Compared to written surveys, they allow you to ask more complex questions, permit clarification of both questions and responses, and enable the interviewer to ask follow-up questions. On the down side, face-to-face interviews are the most expensive of the three options in terms of time, money, and confidentiality (especially in group settings). The quality of results depends on the interviewer's skill in asking questions and in recording responses accurately and completely.

3. Telephone Interviews

   Telephone interviews ideally are short (around 10 minutes), but may last up to 30 minutes. Though still an issue, confidentiality concerns can be addressed to some extent. If responses are short, the interviews may go faster than a written survey. The cost is somewhere between the costs of the other two methods. On the down side, the short timeframe limits the number of questions that can be asked and answered, and long-winded responses further reduce the number of topics that can be addressed.

Once you develop a plan to maintain the integrity of the survey process and select the appropriate survey method, you are ready to address issues related to your survey sample.

Chapter 5: Survey Sample: Size and Other Considerations

Insider Tip: The sample must be representative of the target population.

While the number of respondents does matter, it usually is not the most important characteristic of a survey sample. The extent to which you can generalize your findings to the target population depends more on how representative the sample is of the population and how precise your results must be than it does on how many people are included.

First let's define some terms. **Population** means the total collection of people or elements about which you want to make some inferences. **Sample** means a sub-set of the people or elements in the population. A sample is **representative** of the population when its relevant characteristics (age, gender, income, etc.) are the same as, or not significantly different from, those found in the population. For example, a business owner who wants to know whether to add a retirement program to its benefits package surveys her employees. If 20 of the 25 respondents are over 40 years old, but older workers comprise only 10% of the workforce, the sample is not representative.

Precision, which refers to the level of accuracy you want or need for your results, is another important determinant of sample size. Because it is unlikely that the sample will mirror the population exactly, there will be some level of sampling error. Thus the higher the desired level of precision, the larger the sample must be. Similarly, the greater the variance in the population (e.g., in terms of difference of opinion, experience, demographics), the larger the sample must be to provide the designated level of accuracy.

Sample size also depends on the type of data you are collecting – quantitative (numerical) or qualitative (narrative). There are rules about sample size for quantitative data to ensure statistically reliable results. The more complex the data, or the more you want to sub-divide the data, the larger the required sample size. For example, if you are going to segment the data by demographic characteristics, each segment must have a minimum number of responses. Qualitative data, on the other hand, are not subject to the same rules. Instead, the validity of the findings is determined by the usefulness and logic of the data.

Surveys are generally conducted using samples rather than populations because including fewer people makes the survey more cost effective and requires less time; the population is not always known or accessible; and a representative sample provides essentially the same results. Populations may be used if (a) they are small, (b) there are legitimate reasons to have everyone participate, (c) there is a wide diversity of opinion, or (d) the sample is not representative.

If you don't have enough people in your sample, it's possible that your results will be unreliable. For example, one divergent response out of five has a much bigger impact than one out of fifty. What can you do? First, try to increase the sample size. If you have some concerns about a small sample or low response rate ahead of time, try to expand the initial sample and/or identify effective techniques to increase the response rate. (See Chapter 17 for ideas about how to maximize the response rate.) Second, you might be able to mediate the effects of small sample size somewhat through the statistics you choose: for instance, use the median values instead of the mean.

When you have a small sample, it is even more important that you ensure respondents' privacy. Individuals may fear that decision makers will be able to identify their responses, which will deter them from participating. One way to address this concern is to combine response categories when reporting results. For example, if you are surveying work groups with 10 or fewer members, you can combine the responses of two or more of the groups for reporting purposes. Of course, let respondents know in advance that you will do this, as it might have a positive influence their decision to participate.

In short, while the size of your sample does matter, it is not necessarily the ruling characteristic. Representativeness is a key factor; the level of accuracy also is a consideration. Your best bet is to identify a sample that is large enough for your purposes and will provide statistically significant results.

Chapter 6: Communication Issues

Insider Tip: Communication must be an integral part
of the survey process.

Developing and implementing an effective communication plan are key elements of a successful survey process. Communication throughout the survey process should be formalized in an action plan. Content should include what is communicated, by whom, to whom, when, how, how often, why, and in what format(s). Try to anticipate stakeholders' questions and answer them in advance. Accountability is critical to the success of the communication plan.

Good communication plays a key role in demonstrating the fairness of the survey process. For example, potential ethical dilemmas should be addressed, beforehand if possible, and the decisions communicated. Information such as who will have access to the data and how privacy issues will be handled should be made early and communicated clearly. There is a huge payoff to a procedurally fair process. Stakeholders will accept decisions based on the results, even adverse or undesirable ones, if they believe that the process that gave rise to those results was fair. Thus you should ensure that your survey process is transparent, free of bias, and allows for input from those affected by it.

Here are some communication issues that often are ignored or overlooked in surveys:

Who:
Senior management and other influential people must communicate with survey stakeholders in order to generate a sense of importance and urgency. While there should be one clearly identified executive advocate of the survey process, others need to be involved as well. For example, there should be a letter from the appropriate executive announcing the impending survey as well as a cover letter signed by him/her that accompanies the survey instrument.

What:
Issues to be communicated include the following:
- The purpose of the survey
- Who is involved and what their roles are
- Why people should participate (i.e., "What's in it for me?")
- How the results will be used
- Confidentiality and privacy assurances
- How the process will unfold
- Timing and deadlines
- Who will receive the results and in what format (e.g., summary, full report)
- The findings
- What changes occurred, or will occur, as a result of the findings

Why:
Communication plays a key role in a survey process that is perceived as procedurally fair. In the absence of information, people are likely to fill the vacuum by making

unwarranted assumptions that will cause unnecessary headaches for everyone involved.

When:
Communication with your stakeholders, and especially with your target audience, must be consistent throughout the survey process. You cannot communicate too much. In addition, you must follow up six to twelve months later and report the changes that occurred as a result of the findings.

How:
Use a variety of media to address different learning styles: written, verbal, and online systems. For a large-scale and/or big impact survey, you might consider providing resources such as frequently asked questions on an intranet that people can access at their convenience, and/or a video that is widely available.

Throughout the survey process, honesty is the best policy. This is especially true if the data indicate unanticipated problems or negative responses. Management's credibility is on the line if negative results are hidden or withheld. Once trust is lost or broken, it is difficult to restore.

Insider Secret:
Six to twelve months after the survey, you need to close the loop by assessing what changes have been made and reporting those changes to stakeholders. Be sure to link the changes specifically to the survey's findings so people know that their voices were heard. Few organizations take this final step, yet it is key to the effectiveness of the survey process. (See Chapter 24 for more information on this point.)

Now that you have completed planning the survey process, it's time to design the survey instrument.

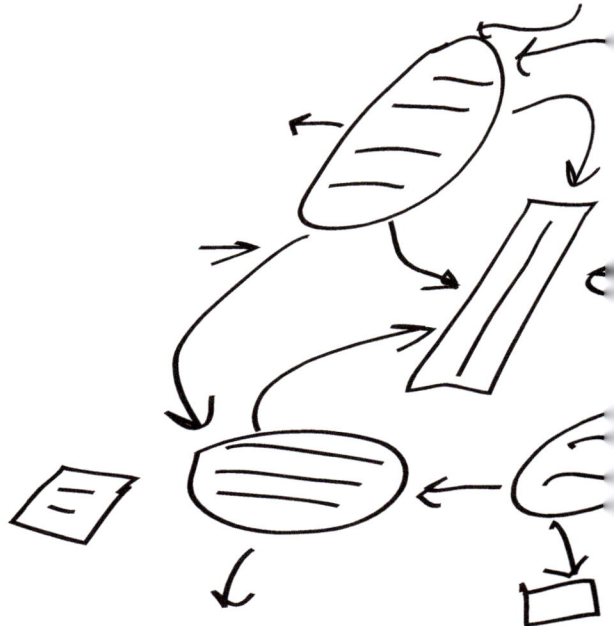

Part 2:

Designing the Survey Instrument

Chapter 7: Survey Design Logistics

Insider Tip: Conducting a pilot survey is one of the best actions you can take.

Although dealing with the logistics of survey design sounds boring, you would be well served to pay attention to them. In most cases, you won't get a chance later on to add something that you didn't address in the design stage. Here are eight of the most important issues that often are overlooked during the design stage:

1. **Timing**
   The best time to conduct your survey depends on factors such as what else is going on, how high a priority the survey is for you and for respondents, and when people are available. Make the response deadline relatively short. A survey whose deadline is a week away is less likely to be relegated to the bottom of the To-Do list.

2. **Length of the Survey**
   The desire to keep the survey relatively short to increase the response rate should be balanced with the purpose of the survey. You need to collect enough information to address the issues at hand or you're wasting the opportunity. Some people will agree to take a longer survey if there is an incentive for doing so, such as gaining access to survey results.

3. **Language**
   Minimize the use of acronyms and abbreviations, and use terms that everyone is likely to recognize and define the same way. For example, always define terms like "supervisor" and "senior management." When in doubt, define your terms. Make sure that the reading level is appropriate to the audience; a survey should not be a literacy test.

4. **Survey Introduction**
   The introduction is a key aspect of a survey. In order to increase its effectiveness, clearly state the purpose(s) of the survey, explain what's in it for people to participate, what the deadline is, how respondents' confidentiality will be protected, what will be done with the results, and how respondents should return their surveys. Keep the introduction as short and simple as possible while including the necessary information. Tell people how you want them to respond (e.g., check the boxes, write in the responses). Provide contact information so they can ask questions. Don't forget to thank them for their participation!

5. **Method of Survey Administration**
   The method by which you deliver the survey and receive the results has implications for your survey's design. Options include paper and pencil (face to-face or private), online, e-mail, and even mobile phone. Be sure to clearly address how the results are to be returned and to whom, whether it's someone in-house or an outside expert. In making your choices, consider factors such as participants' comfort level with the method, ease of access to relevant technology,

and confidentiality concerns. Also remember that you must pay employees for the time spent completing a survey. Thus you may want to administer it onsite during work hours to avoid having to pay overtime.

6. **Response Rate**

   Here are a few ideas about how to maximize your response rate during the design stage. Identify a top executive who will be an active advocate for the survey, and have that executive communicate the purpose of the survey ahead of time. Write a cover letter for his/her signature that will accompany the survey. Let people know ahead of time the survey's purpose, how the results will be used, and the benefit of completing the survey. Get managers on board to support the survey and encourage their employees to respond. For other suggestions on maximizing your response rate, see Chapter 17.

7. **How to Use the Results**

   The design stage is the point at which you need to decide what you will do with the data once you receive them, and what types of data analysis will provide the answers that decision-makers can use easily to take action.

8. **Pilot Survey**

   Before you launch the survey, it's a good idea to pre-test it with a small group that is representative of the population you will be sampling. By soliciting feedback and revising the survey accordingly, you will avoid unnecessary confusion and/or frustration that otherwise could skew the results or reduce your response rate.

Tending to these issues during the design stage will save you headaches later and increase the effectiveness of the survey process.

Chapter 8: Preparing to Write Effective Survey Questions

Insider Tip: Survey items are critical; poorly written questions result in unusable data.

The importance of effective survey questions cannot be overemphasized. Simply stated, poorly written questions result in unusable data. The quality, reliability, and validity of the survey items are critical to eliciting accurate and actionable information from the respondents. Yet questions often are the weakest or even most harmful element of a survey.

Each item must be assessed relative to the survey's purpose. You should ask only for information that you will actually use and that can provide you with meaningful and actionable results. For example, you should collect demographic data (work location, tenure on the job, job title, etc.) only if they will enable you to take action. If results indicate dissatisfaction with supervisors for instance, knowing which locations are reporting problems would help you target your response.

As you write the survey items, remind yourself what information you want to obtain and how you plan to use it. For example, do you want to know what your customers think about your service levels, or what employees think about their work environment? Once you know the answers, what, exactly, do you plan to do with that information?

Here are eight additional issues you must address as you prepare to write questions:

1. Type of Data
   Will the users of your survey results be best served by numerical (quantitative) or by narrative (qualitative) data, or by a combination of the two?

2. Type of Questions
   Who knew there are so many varieties of questions? Some of your choices are open vs. closed-ended, single-item (global) vs. scales, and quantitative vs. qualitative. See Chapters 9 and 10 to learn about the pros and cons of these types of questions.

3. Relevance of Items
   How exactly is each item or scale related to the purpose of the survey? Will it allow you to answer your specific questions?

4. Integrity of Data
   How do you know that the information being gathered is reliable and measures what you think it does? See Chapters 13 and 14 to learn Insider Secrets about the critical roles of reliability and validity.

5. Level of Privacy Provided

   Will your survey process provide anonymity or confidentiality for respondents? **Anonymity** means those who receive the results have no idea who participated in the survey. This level of privacy is nearly impossible to achieve in an organizational setting. **Confidentiality** means the results cannot be attributed to any given individual. Be clear about how you will provide the appropriate level of privacy.

6. Use of Demographic Data

   Do you truly have a need for demographic data? If not, do not ask questions that respondents could perceive as enabling others to identify them. If you do need the information, be sure the survey instructions explain clearly how it will be used, and how respondents' identities will be protected. See Chapter 9 for additional discussion of demographic questions.

7. Clarity of Instructions

   Are the instructions succinct and clear? For example:

   A. Did you explain exactly how you want respondents to indicate the appropriate response (e.g., circle the answer, write the answer, check the box, or provide multiple answers)?

   B. Did you define all relevant terms used in the survey? For example, "The term 'Supervisor' refers to your immediate boss, regardless of his/her actual title."

8. Additional Opportunity to be Heard

   Did you include one or two open-ended questions at the end of the survey? While not mandatory, providing respondents a chance to provide clarifying and/or additional information often yields valuable details that otherwise would have been lost. Here are two examples:

   A. "What else would you like to add?"

   B. "What have I forgotten to ask that would help me get the complete picture?"

The time spent addressing the above issues will pay off by dramatically increasing the usefulness of your survey data.

Chapter 9: Types of Questions - Part I

Insider Tip: Closed-ended questions limit the amount of useful information you can obtain.

The types of questions you choose will have an impact on the effectiveness of your survey. To help guide your decisions, this chapter and the next contain brief descriptions of some common types of questions, an example of each, and some representative strengths and weaknesses.

Quantitative or Closed-Ended Questions

Description:
Quantitative or closed-ended questions are those whose answers are "countable" and can be assigned a number, such as an average score. For example, asking respondents to use a 5-point scale to answer the question, "What is the highest level of education you have achieved as of today?" enables you to provide quantitative results such as frequencies and averages.

Strengths:
- Survey can be completed quickly
- Survey can cover many topics in a short time
- Respondents find it easy to respond
- Data analysis is relatively easy
- Results can be compared due to standardized response options
- These questions can be the most efficient way of gathering certain information like demographic data

Weaknesses:
- Answers may be of limited use in taking action - e.g., you may learn there is a problem but not know why it's an issue
- Response options that do not fit the question could skew the results - for example, a question asks about the level of satisfaction with a topic but only offers options to agree or disagree
- Respondents may become frustrated if forced to choose among answers that don't seem to fit - e.g., there is no "neutral" option, but that's the true answer
- No clarification of questions or answers is possible

Qualitative or Open-Ended Questions

Description:
Qualitative or open-ended questions are those whose answers are descriptive and cannot be reduced to numbers. For example, asking, "What suggestions do you have for improving the performance evaluation process?" will result in a variety of answers. While it's possible to categorize the answers, assigning each one a unique identifier is meaningless.

Strengths:
- Narrative data provide rich, actionable information
- Narrative data tell the stories behind the numbers
- Respondents often feel they are heard when they use their own words
- You may get answers to relevant issues you didn't consider

Weaknesses:
- Survey completion time increases
- Written responses generally require more thought than check-the-box items
- People may vent in inappropriate ways
- The quality of the responses depends on respondents' communication skills
- Data analysis time increases significantly
- A large amount of information collected may be irrelevant
- The data analyst must have the skill to interpret the results accurately

Demographic Questions

Description:
Demographic questions are those that require respondents to divulge descriptive characteristics about themselves that may enable others to identify them. Examples are questions about age, work location, tenure with the organization, and ethnicity.

Strengths:
- Collecting demographic information enables precise analysis that can dramatically increase the usefulness of the results
- You can test for meaningful differences between sub-groups in the sample (e.g., men vs. women, older workers vs. younger ones, one work location vs. another) that will allow you to target your responses

Weaknesses:
- Asking respondents to provide demographic data may lower the response rate due to concerns about privacy, confidentiality, and how the information will be used, particularly in low-trust environments
- There is a potential for abusing the data through discrimination or pinpointing particular respondents

In addition to the above types of questions, there are two other options that must be carefully considered because of their implications on survey effectiveness. We turn to them in the next chapter.

Chapter 10: Types of Questions - Part 2

Insider Tip: Single questions meant to address complex issues do not provide actionable information.

A critical choice in identifying items for your survey is whether to use a single question to address a given issue or topic rather than a scale, which is a series of similar and related questions. While the use of single questions is prevalent in many organizational surveys, it often is inappropriate and misleading.

For example, employers often want to know if workers are satisfied with their jobs, since job satisfaction results in positive organizational outcomes such as employee engagement. A question they may pose on a survey is, "To what extent are you satisfied with your job?" while providing response options that range from very dissatisfied to very satisfied. The problem is that job satisfaction is a complex issue that includes components such as pay, working conditions, supervisors, co-workers, autonomy, and level of responsibility. As a result, when employees answer this question, it's impossible to tell what aspect(s) of their jobs they are thinking about when they respond. This makes the answers unreliable. More importantly, the responses don't allow the employers to take action.

Using a scale is an alternative that provides more specific results that enable decision makers to take appropriate action. In the case of job satisfaction, for example, the scale items would address some of issues listed above. As a result, employers would learn about overall job satisfaction as well as which aspects may be problematic.

Single-Item or "Global" Questions

Description:
Single-item or "global" questions are meant to address an entire issue or topic single-handedly. For example, "How satisfied are you with your supervisor?" is meant to elicit one answer to a multi-faceted issue. (The alternative to asking a global question is to use a scale, described below.)

Strengths:
- The survey can be shorter, or it can cover more topics in the same length of time as a survey that includes scales
- Global questions are sometimes appropriate
- The items can provide useful information if included at the end of a scale

Weaknesses:
- Responses often are not actionable because the topics they are intended to assess are complex
- Decision makers inaccurately assume the results provide a comprehensive answer

Scales

Description:

Scales are a series of closely related questions meant to address various facets of a complex issue or topic. The number of items may range from two or three to twenty or more. For example, a well-known scale that addresses satisfaction with one's supervisor contains nineteen behavioral questions. Analysis provides information about the overall "satisfaction with my supervisor" rating as well as about each of the individual items.

Strengths:
- Results generally are much more accurate, useful, and actionable than global items
- Actions can target specific behaviors or outcomes

Weaknesses:
- Surveys take longer to complete because of the number of questions
- Respondents sometimes question why they are asked to respond to similar items
- The data analyst must have the skills to interpret the data

Now that you know the Insider Secrets about writing questions that provide accurate, actionable information, it's time to turn your attention to the other part of survey questions that novices often overlook: the response options.

Chapter II: Anchors or Response Options

Insider Tip: Confusing response options decrease
the reliability of survey results.

The answers provided for each question, called **response options** or **anchors**, are important elements in the survey instrument. They should make it easy for respondents to provide accurate answers. Below are answers to four frequently asked questions about response options, followed by a list of seven tips to dramatically increase the reliability of your survey results.

1. What is the optimal number of response options for each question?

    Five options are appropriate for most surveys, although some people opt for seven. Research shows most people are unable to make meaningful distinctions when there are more than nine choices. The answer for you depends on how you intend to use the survey results. For example, if you need to determine the order in which potential benefits should be offered, five or seven anchors will enable you to make meaningful interpretations, whereas three response options may not provide fine enough distinctions.

2. Should you have an odd number of anchors or an even number?

    An odd number is preferable, though one could justify either choice. An even number of anchors generally omits a "neutral" response, forcing people to choose between positive or negative. The fact is that sometimes people genuinely do feel neutral about an issue, so forcing them to choose an incorrect response will skew the results. In addition, some people feel frustrated when the survey structure does not permit them to give a truthful answer, which may cause them to stop the survey or not take it seriously.

3. Is it better for anchors to be numbers or descriptive words?

    For the best results, provide descriptive words or phrases instead of, or in addition to, numbers. This will increase the reliability of responses, as respondents are more likely to have a consistent "picture" of each one. If you use a numbered scale, the highest number should consistently be the most positive response Similarly, descriptive anchors should consistently be listed from negative to positive.

    Although an improvement over numbers alone, providing words for only the high and low anchors (e.g., 1 = very dissatisfied and 5 = very satisfied) is not sufficient The data may be unreliable because there is no way to determine respondents' understanding of undefined options 2, 3, and 4. Take the time to write out the descriptions for ALL the anchors.

4. What are some examples of common "descriptive" anchors?
    - Degree of satisfaction or dissatisfaction
    - Extent of agreement or disagreement

- Degree of importance
- Frequency
- Intention to act or not act

Here are seven additional tips about response options that will make the difference between valid and invalid results. Make sure that:

1. Anchors are grammatically correct and consistent with the questions asked. When the nature of the questions changes (e.g., from "How satisfied are you with …?" to "To what extent do you agree that…?"), so must your anchors.

2. Response options are parallel and have a logical progression.

3. Anchors are clearly distinguishable. For example, if respondents are unable to differentiate between responses like "often" and "frequently," or "few" and "several," or "sometimes" and "occasionally," your results will be unreliable.

4. Response categories are non-overlapping. For example, 1-50 and 50-100 are overlapping categories.

5. There are no absolutes. Because few things or conditions are "always" or "never" true or untrue, using those words could skew the results.

6. You move all common words to the question to avoid unnecessary repetition in the responses. This list is a good example of this tip. Note how the words "Make sure that" appear in the explanatory paragraph instead of being repeated in every item. Common survey words that should be part of the items instead of the anchors are, "the" and "a/an."

7. Avoid bias in response options such as the one in this example:

    Who contributed most to the poor quality of the training program?
    A. Instructors
    B. Counselors
    C. High-paid managers who run the centers

Ensuring that your response options are clear, consistent, and logical is an easy way to boost the usefulness of your survey results.

Chapter 12: Tips for Writing Effective Questions

Insider Tip: Each question should relate directly to the purpose of the survey.

1. Use neutral language, i.e., no leading questions that convey or suggest a desired response. Ask, "What did you think about this program?" instead of "Was this a good program?"

2. Be as objective as possible; avoid emotionally laden questions.

3. Avoid social bias or social desirability items such as, "Most employees contributed to the United Way campaign. To what extent do you intend to contribute as well?"

4. State questions in the affirmative. If there is no way to avoid asking a negative question, draw attention to the negative word (e.g., "not") by capitalizing it or using bold font. Avoid using double negatives.

5. Ask one question or topic per item. When you ask multiple questions in one item, you have no way of knowing which ones respondents are answering. Asking employees to indicate the extent of their agreement or disagreement with the statement, "The CEO is doing a really good job and treating employees well," is an example of asking two questions in one item. Instead, write two separate questions.

6. Use open-ended questions or those that can be answered along a continuum (e.g., from strongly disagree to strongly agree) rather than questions that require a yes or no, or single word answer. With a few exceptions (demographic data, for example), single word answers provide little, if any, usable information.

7. The questions should be written clearly and succinctly, without extraneous information. Include only the information necessary to provide an accurate response.

8. Each item should relate to the purpose of the survey. Those that are off-point raise unnecessary questions about the survey's credibility.

9. Use the language of the organization but avoid unnecessary abbreviations, acronyms, or slang. It's possible that some respondents will not know them or be able to identify them correctly. If you absolutely have to use such terms, define them clearly the first time you use them.

10. Define your terms. For example, "The term Supervisor is defined as the person to whom you report directly, regardless of that individual's actual title."

11. Avoid "extreme" words (e.g., all, none, always, never). Generally there will be exceptions to these terms, so the correct response automatically will be "no."

12. The reading level of the items should be appropriate for your respondents. Unless your purpose is to test respondents' reading ability, the vocabulary should be as basic as necessary.

13. Use gender-neutral language.

14. Pay attention to the precision of your words. Ensure they have unambiguous meanings. If they do not, define or describe them, or give brief relevant examples.

15. Write the questions using a conversational tone. Use the active voice.

16. Follow the rules of grammar. Sentence structure should be simple and direct. For example, avoid multiple prepositional phrases, and put subject and verb close together.

17. Make sure it's clear what adjectives go with which nouns, and which pronouns go with which people. Use parallel structure to make sure subjects and verbs are consistent (i.e., both singular or both plural).

18. Don't make the questions personal unless you want an opinion. For example, "What would you do if…?" asks for an opinion. Asking "What should a supervisor do if…?" requires knowledge of a standard policy or practice.

19. Make sure the questions are clear to the respondents and that the words communicate the intended question accurately.

The easier it is for people to read and understand survey questions, the more likely it is that the answers will be reliable, accurate, and complete.

Chapter 13: Why Reliability Matters

Insider Tip: Survey items that are reliable produce consistent, dependable information.

Survey results are meaningless unless the survey questions consistently measure what you think they are measuring. Reliability and validity are the tools used to assess these two critical determinants of survey effectiveness; ignore them at your peril. We discuss reliability in this chapter and validity in Chapter 14.

Reliability refers to the consistency or dependability of your survey items. An easy way to understand this concept is to think of a bathroom scale, a tool used to measure people's weight. A scale is considered consistent or reliable if you get about the same number when you step on the scale, note the number indicated, step off the scale, then repeat this procedure several times. A reliable scale also is consistent over time – i.e., absent any changes in your habits such as significantly increasing or decreasing your food intake, the number it shows remains stable. Similarly, when you ask the same or similar questions on a survey, you want respondents to provide essentially the same answer each time. If this is the case, the questions are said to be reliable and the answers they provide are dependable.

But what if you don't get consistent answers to a survey question? Either the item is unreliable (e.g., too broad, vague, or confusing as written), in which case you cannot depend on the answers you get, or something has changed. When things ARE supposed to change – for example, skills improve after training – then you would expect answers to reflect the new circumstances. However, when things are not supposed to change – how supervisors treat employees, for example, or the quality of service provided – inconsistent answers indicate a problem that must be addressed.

Here are answers to two common reliability issues:

1. **How can you increase the reliability of your survey responses?**
   One way is to use scales instead of single questions. A scale in this context consists of a series of questions that address the same concept or issue in slightly different yet related ways. (See Chapter 10 for a discussion of single items and scales.) For example, instead of asking a single question to assess employees' satisfaction with their supervisor (e.g., "To what extent are you satisfied with your supervisor?"), you can use a scale developed to assess that concept via a series of related questions. By including a number of items that are related to the concept being measured (as determined through scale development statistical methods), you can increase the level of reliability of the items. As an added bonus, scores on each item in the scale can be used to pinpoint specific areas that need attention, something a single question cannot do.

2. **How do you know whether specific questions or scales are reliable?**
   This is one area where survey expertise is critical. People who have been trained in survey and test development can research the reliability of the items or, for single item questions, they can ensure the items are written in ways that produce

consistent responses. While following the tips in Chapter 12 is a good start to obtaining consistent results, it's best to consult an expert about the reliability of your survey items.

Although reliability is a necessary condition for obtaining accurate and actionable survey results, it is not sufficient. The use of the survey items must also be validated for their intended purpose. The next chapter provides insider tips on validity – i.e., how to make sure your items measure what you think they are measuring.

Chapter 14: How to Increase the Survey's Accuracy

Insider Tip: Unless the use of your survey items has been validated, you can't be sure what you're measuring.

In measurement, **validity** addresses the question of whether a tool or instrument measures what we think it is measuring. In an employee or customer survey, validity tells us whether and how well we are measuring the concept, topic or issue we think we are measuring. As an example, let's return to the bathroom scale analogy. People purchase a scale because they believe it measures their weight at a given point in time. When they use the results in ways that are consistent with this purpose, such as determining the effect of their diet on their weight, we say the use of the bathroom scale has been validated. However, if employers have workers weigh in and then use the results as an indicator of their job satisfaction, the use of the scale has not been validated. Although the tool itself (the scale) has not changed, the intended *use* of the results has changed.

While the above example is nonsensical, it makes the point clearly. The focus must be on how the answers to a given question or scale are *used*, rather than on the questions themselves. This point is critical to understanding the importance of validity in survey development. One of the biggest misconceptions in developing surveys is that questions or scales in and of themselves are valid or invalid. Thus, unsuspecting individuals purchase off-the-shelf survey scales that are described as being valid. It is the USE of the questions that must be examined, not the questions themselves. You must ensure that the items and scales you use are actually intended for the purpose for which you plan to use them. For each question or scale on your survey, you should be clear about two points:

1. What characteristic do you want to measure?

2. How well does this question/scale measure that characteristic?

Your responses will determine whether you will be able to obtain accurate, actionable information.

Another example of how a misunderstanding of validity can provide misleading and inaccurate results is the all too common error that occurs when people use global questions to assess a complex issue, believing the responses give them an accurate answer. For example, general agreement that one's job is satisfactory may mask widespread disparities about satisfaction with specific facets of the job. Perhaps an employee thinks the pay and benefits are good but the workload and the supervisor are terrible, and therefore gives a "compromise" response to the global question. The employer will think all is well, when in reality it's possible the employee will leave because dissatisfaction with one's immediate supervisor is the #1 reason why workers quit their jobs.

It is possible to have reliability without validity. However, effective surveys must have both. The items must be reliable and their use must be validated. Here are two vital questions to ask yourself:

1. Can you draw accurate conclusions based on the answers to the survey items?

2. How well does each item allow you to assess a given issue?

If your answers are, respectively, "yes" and "very well," then you are setting yourself up for success.

Now that you have planned the survey process and designed the survey instrument, it's time to move to the survey administration stage.

Part 3:

Administering the Survey

Chapter 15: Survey Administration Logistics

Insider Tip: Non-exempt employees must be paid for the time spent completing a survey.

Although many of the logistical and technical issues have been addressed during the planning and design stages, a few remain during the administration stage. Here are seven issues that must be addressed or checked at this point:

1. **Technical Support**
   If there are glitches in an online or e-mail survey administration, do you have someone either in-house or from the vendor who is available to correct them immediately? Can you do a trial run before the survey goes "live?"

2. **Tracking Responses**
   Is there a legitimate reason for you to be able to track who responded? If so, be sure the appropriate coding is in place. For example, each survey may be assigned a unique identifier or code that can be checked off when the survey is completed. Online systems usually allow you to track surveys; be sure you understand what's required for you to use this feature. (See Chapter 16 for information about how to choose an online survey vendor.)

3. **Privacy**
   Double-check to ensure that all privacy-related protections are in place as promised. For example, if you code the surveys, ensure that the person receiving the data does not have access to the master list that connects the codes to individuals. The only person who needs to see the raw data is the data analyst. If you use paper and pencil surveys, be sure there is a secure place to store them. Make sure that you are able to deliver the promised level of privacy to respondents.

4. **Payment for Employees**
   Non-exempt employees must be paid for the time they spend completing a survey. If you want to avoid paying them overtime, make sure they complete the survey during their normal work hours. While exempt employees do not receive overtime, you can increase survey response rates by allowing them to complete their surveys during their regular working hours rather than on their own time.

5. **In-Person Administration**
   When surveys are administered in person, provide a setting and time period that allow respondents to feel comfortable and not rushed. For example, people sitting elbow to elbow are not likely to feel their answers are private. Have extra copies of the survey and bring pens for those who have none. Allow the respondents to deposit their surveys in unmarked envelopes and hand them directly to a third party. Supervisors and managers should NOT be present.

6. **Returning the Surveys**

   Make sure that respondents know exactly how to return their completed surveys. If the surveys are online, for example, can they stop at some point and return to the task later without losing their responses to date?

7. **Follow Up**

   Research and experience show that following up appropriately on surveys can dramatically boost response rates. Most online survey vendors offer an option for automatic follow up. Paper and pencil or e-mail surveys require you to do more work to create an effective tracking process.

Online vendors can handle many of the logistical issues that arise during the administrative stage. However, since the available options vary considerably, you need to be certain you know exactly what services and features you are purchasing. The next chapter suggests some criteria to use when selecting an online survey vendor.

Chapter 16: How to Choose an online Survey Vendor

Insider Tip: Distinguish clearly between "must have" features and "nice to have" ones.

More and more organizations are leveraging technology to help in the administration, analysis and reporting stages of a survey. You can choose from a range of vendor services, from survey administration only, to data analysis, to reporting. Your needs may vary from survey to survey, so plan ahead when shopping for a vendor.

Step 1: Identify the criteria that are important and will make the administration and analysis of the surveys as easy as possible for your respondents, as well as for you. The criteria may depend in part on the expertise of the person managing the survey, who ideally will also be involved in the vendor selection.

Step 2: Prioritize the criteria. Distinguish clearly between "must have," "nice to have," and "interesting or flashy but don't need" elements. Make sure you have ALL your "must have" elements and NONE of your "don't need" elements.

Step 3: Select a vendor. Use the list below to identify the questions that must be answered to ensure you fully understand the vendor's system. Use your prioritized list to check that the system has all of your "must have" elements. Be sure to analyze the customer service.

Here are twelve sample criteria for choosing an online vendor:

1. Ease of Use
   The system should be easy to use both for the administrator and respondents.

2. Compatibility
   Is the vendor's product (software, program, system) compatible with your hardware?

3. Data Management
   How easy is it to download the data to other programs for analysis (e.g., statistical software such as SPSS, Excel)? Do the data download easily and accurately, or must you do a lot of "cleanup" work before you can use them?

4. Data Analysis Capability
   Purchase only what you actually need, which is driven by the purpose(s) of the survey(s). If simple analyses are sufficient for the foreseeable future, there is no need to purchase a package that supports more complex levels of analysis.

5. Import/Export Capability
   Do you want to be able to conduct the analyses within the survey system, or do you want to export the data to a different and/or existing system (e.g., SPSS)?

6. Privacy
   How are data privacy issues handled? You must address privacy issues from the

respondents' point of view as well as from the organization's point of view. Be sure you get answers to questions such as these:

A. How can you be sure the data will be secure and seen only by those authorized to see them?

B. Will the data be encrypted?

C. Will the identifying information be stripped before the data are seen by those who might be able to determine the identity of respondents? This factor is especially important in employee surveys.

7. **Range of Question Types**
Does the vendor provide the types of questions you need? Can you add your own questions or must you use prewritten items? Are all types of questions supported by the vendor's data analysis programs?

8. **Ability to Customize**
Are you able to insert your organization's logo on the survey and reports? This issue is especially important for customer surveys. Can you make the changes yourself or must you rely on the vendor to make them for you?

9. **Customer Support**
Can you get the support you need easily whenever you need it? Be sure to evaluate the user friendliness of the vendor's support staff.

10. **Report Capabilities**
Is the system capable of generating the necessary reports in the form(s) that best suits your needs? Are the reports customizable? If so, how long will it take and who must do it?

11. **Limitations**
Are there limits on the number of questions permitted per survey, the number of respondents, or the number of surveys permitted in a given time period (e.g., month, quarter, year)?

12. **Cost**
While cost is important, it should not be the driving force behind your decision. Better you should spend a little more than you want and get exactly what you need than to end up with a system that doesn't do the job.

If you conduct surveys infrequently, there is no need for you to purchase a survey software system. Simply outsource everything to a survey expert who has access to the necessary tools.

Chapter 17: How to Maximize Your Survey Response Rate

Insider Tip: Significantly boosting your response rate requires advance planning.

The **survey response rate** is calculated as the number of usable surveys returned (i.e., those completed correctly) divided by the number of surveys distributed. The survey response rate is important because it affects the survey's credibility and the usefulness of the findings. If you have too few responses, the results are easily skewed, making them unreliable. There are two important aspects of response rates addressed here: the percentage of usable responses and the representativeness of the data.

The number of usable responses is especially important for a quantitative survey because the analysis requires a minimum number of data points in order for the results to be reliable. More than this minimum may be required for the results to be representative. In research studies, response rates in the 30% range are often considered good. Using some of the techniques below, you can increase your response rates significantly into the 70-80% range. For qualitative surveys, there is a non-numerical rule of thumb: continue collecting data until you can identify specific patterns.

When the survey sample is representative of the population from which it is drawn, you can have a high degree of confidence that you would get about the same results if you surveyed the entire population. When you have a diverse population, it's particularly important that you obtain the responses needed to determine whether there are meaningful distinctions among them. For example, suppose a city conducts a survey to solicit public opinion about how to prioritize services. If 750 of 1000 surveys returned are from city workers whose objective is to keep their jobs, yet such workers comprise only 2% of the city's population, the survey results are not likely to be representative of residents' preferences. In this case, the city must increase the number of responses from non-employees.

In addition to the steps identified earlier in the design stage of the survey process (see Chapter 7 on design stage logistics), you can take additional actions during the administrative stage to increase the response rate. Here are ten suggestions:

1. Provide a cover letter from a high-level executive that asks people to respond, telling them how important it is that their voices be heard.

2. Ensure the confidentiality safeguards are in place.

3. Be sure the introduction to the survey covers these points:
   - The purpose of the survey
   - How the results will be used
   - How respondents' confidentiality will be protected

- What's in it for respondents to complete the survey
- Instructions for completing and submitting the survey
- The deadline
- Contact information of someone who can answer questions

4. Make it easy for respondents to complete the survey by following the guidelines provided in this booklet about writing questions and responses. In general, make sure the questions are easy to understand and answer, and that the response options are not confusing.

5. Reduce concerns about privacy and possible retaliation by having the results sent directly to an outside third party.

6. Make the entire process as transparent as possible.

7. For workplace surveys, consider administering the survey in person during a meeting when all employees are present. For customer surveys, ask people to complete them on the spot.

8. Make it easy for people to return their surveys. For example, in the case of paper and pencil instruments, provide a stamped, self-addressed envelope.

9. Provide incentives. The most common one is offering to share a summary of the results with those who wish to see them. Sometimes respondents have the opportunity to win a prize from among those who participate, or everyone who responds may receive a small gift. If you offer incentives, be sure they are things the respondents value.

10. Engage in multiple follow-ups. The forms they take depend in part on the method by which the survey was administered. The follow-ups should be a combination of a reminder to return the survey if they haven't done so already, and a thank you for their time and effort.

Receiving a sufficient number of completed usable surveys is key to obtaining actionable data. Most response-boosting techniques require advance planning, yet require little or no additional cost.

Chapter 18: Ethical Issues

Insider Tip: When you conduct a study, you have
a duty to protect participants' privacy.

When you decide to conduct a survey, whether it's of your employees or your customers, you take on the responsibility for protecting the participants' privacy. In some countries, such as those in the European Union, there are legal obligations to protect individuals' privacy, so be sure you are familiar with them. Many of the requirements represent good business practices, so you may want to take a look at them and adopt those that make sense for your organization. You would be well advised to develop a written policy about the ethical practices to be strictly followed when developing and administering surveys.

Below are five privacy-related issues that survey administrators have an ethical obligation to address. Though some of them have been addressed in other chapters, we view them here from an ethical perspective.

1. Communicating the Level of Privacy
    Think of privacy as a continuum that ranges from responses that are anonymous to responses that are public. While we seldom see either of those extreme levels of privacy, they are options. Most often the best that survey administrators can do is promise confidentiality, which falls somewhere in the middle.

    Confidentiality means that while others may know who was included in the survey sample, individuals' responses cannot be attributed to them. While designing safeguards for privacy is relatively easy for a written survey to be taken in private, it is more challenging for surveys administered verbally or in group settings simply because other people see who is there and hear the responses. It is critical that you correctly identify the level of privacy and then ensure it is provided. Be honest, even if it means that some people will choose not to participate.

2. Providing the Promised Level of Privacy
    How will you ensure that the confidentiality promised to respondents will be maintained? You need to articulate, in advance, the process by which the data will be protected, and communicate this process to potential respondents. They are the ones who must be comfortable that you will do as you have promised. If there is a low level of trust in your organization, have an outside expert manage the survey process.

3. Accessing the Data
    Who will be allowed to see the raw data, including data that may contain identifying information? Access should be limited strictly to those who truly have a need to know, which is generally only the individual who will be conducting the data analyses. Respondents need to know in advance who will be able to see the survey data, and for what purpose.

4. Maintaining the Data
   How long will the survey responses be kept? Where will they be stored and how secure will they be? Who will have access to them? One suggestion is to destroy the data and all identifying information after the survey has been completed and the results reported and discussed. (Note: Different advice would be given for data collected for research purposes.)

5. Promising Action
   What are decision makers willing and able to do with the results of the survey? Inherent in conducting a survey is the assumption that there will be some action based on the findings. While leaders have no obligation to do whatever respondents suggest or ask, they have an obligation to take some action. The options range from taking the recommended actions, to letting respondents know their suggestions are being considered by decision makers, to explaining why the organization is unable or unwilling to do as asked.

   The point is that conducting a survey raises expectations of action. If those expectations are not met, the leaders lose credibility and often have to deal with negative workplace or customer consequences. Most top survey experts will not conduct a survey for an organization whose leaders refuse to promise to take action.

Having administered the survey, achieved the desired response rate, and addressed all ethical issues, it's time to analyze the data to learn what respondents had to say.

Part 4:

Analyzing the Data

Chapter 19: Data Entry

Insider Tip: Survey results are constrained by the accuracy of the data that produce them.

Because much of the work in developing successful surveys is done in the planning and design stages, there are fewer logistics to tend to in the later stages. Nonetheless, there are a few issues specific to data entry that must be addressed. Here are seven:

1. Raw data should be entered into the database. That is, there should be no data reduction or combination (e.g., entering average scores instead of actual scores) at this point. Here's why:
   - The possibility of error increases.
   - Such changes may skew the results.
   - You will be unable to retrace the data trail should it become necessary to do so.
   - Based on your preliminary findings, you may decide to perform additional analyses that require the original data.

   The bottom line: prevent unnecessary re-work by saving all data manipulation for the data analysis stage.

2. Data should be entered as they are received. Note: This point is moot if you are using an online survey vendor whose system automatically enters respondents' answers directly into the database. Even in that case, the survey expert should monitor the data so he/she can catch any pertinent information that might require immediate action. If, for example, the surveys being returned are incomplete or unusable, you need to focus on increasing the response rates and/or checking to see if there is a systemic problem. If you discover either of these situations after all the surveys have been returned, it's too late to take corrective action.

3. Data that are imported or exported should be checked for accuracy. Even when one exercises great care in moving data between systems or programs, the fact is that this movement may cause unintended changes. Allocate time and resources to "clean up" the data before you begin the analyses. Do not destroy the original data set, as you may have occasion to refer to it later.

4. Data that are entered by hand and/or scanned should be checked for accuracy. This is the point at which it is easiest to catch and correct errors.

5. Hard copies of surveys should be stored in a safe place after their data have been entered. Access should be strictly limited.

6. The raw data should be accessible on an extremely limited basis. Only those who have a compelling reason to see those data and original surveys should be permitted access. (Note: The access issues should be clarified up front, and the decision implemented during the analysis phase.)

7. If data entry is to be done by hand, identify in advance the specific individual who will enter the data. Ensure there are no conflicts of interest (e.g., a peer of the respondents enters the data, or someone who has a vested interest in the outcome). Go over the survey privacy policy with that person and stress the responsibility required for that task.

    Though on its face, data entry seems like a mundane task, in many ways the integrity of the survey process depends on how, and how well, it is handled. Do not make the mistake of underestimating its importance and the key role it plays.

Chapter 20: Types of Data Analysis

Insider Tip: The type of data prescribes the rules for their analysis.

Data are either quantitative (numerical) or qualitative (narrative). In any given survey you can use one type or a combination. In this section we provide a brief overview of issues to consider when analyzing each type of data, as well as how you can integrate the two of them for optimum results.

To ensure their reliability, validity, and statistical significance, quantitative data are subject to specific rules of analysis that are based on certain assumptions. For example, the category of numbers used (nominal, ordinal, etc.) determines what types of analyses can be performed. There are many ways in which such data may be analyzed; choosing the most appropriate ones depends on the purpose of the study and the extent to which the questions were written to permit the desired analyses. This fact highlights the importance of planning in the survey process. (Chapter 21 describes some common types of statistical analysis for quantitative data.)

In contrast, qualitative data are subject to much less stringent and many fewer rules. Qualitative questions are used to discover the stories behind the numbers, so necessarily the data are non-numeric and not quantifiable. In analyzing these data, one seeks to establish categories, identify relevant patterns, determine the importance of information, determine relationships, identify trends, and prioritize the results. The quality of the analysis depends greatly on the skills of the analyst in interpreting the data, as well as on the skills of the individuals collecting and providing the data.

There are situations in which using both kinds of data is the best alternative. The question then becomes, what is the best way to integrate the two? The answer lies in the purpose of the study. If the purpose is to discover, consider using qualitative results to help define what quantitative data should be gathered. Qualitative data enable you to get inside people's heads, and the findings emerge from the data.

For example, if you don't know what issues are on your employees' or customers' minds, you might conduct focus groups, phone interviews, or written surveys with open-ended questions (e.g., "What's your biggest concern about…?"). In this situation, you might use open-ended questions to discover what's got their attention, and then use targeted quantitative questions to get specific, actionable answers.

However, if the purpose is to understand, qualitative results are best used to help explain the quantitative findings, to explore theories, and to delve more deeply into key issues. If you don't understand the reasons behind quantitative survey responses, you may want to follow up with open-ended questions to learn more and to get the stories behind the numbers.

For instance, one non-profit organization had been using quantitative questions in surveys to evaluate an annual event. The results were of limited use because they didn't tell the story behind the numbers – i.e., they didn't explain why were people satisfied or dissatisfied with certain aspects of their experiences. As a result, the survey was redesigned to ask primarily open-ended questions. By soliciting people's stories about their experiences, the organization was able to fill in the gaps and obtain actionable information to help improve the event.

Some of the disadvantages of using qualitative data are that the analysis requires skill, it is very time consuming, and much of the data will be unusable. You can use tools such as Excel to help sort data and conduct limited analysis. You can also find software programs to analyze qualitative data. However, no matter how good the tools are, the quality of the data are limited by the skill of the data collector. And, you still need a skilled analyst to help interpret the results.

The purpose of your survey determines the type of data that are best suited to provide accurate, actionable information. To the extent your purpose is clear, data analysis decisions are much easier.

Chapter 21: Survey Statistics

Insider Tip: Simple types of data analysis are sufficient for most business surveys.

For most types of business surveys, simple types of data analysis are sufficient to answer the questions the survey is meant to address. The appropriate types of data analysis depend both on the purpose of your study and on the types of questions you ask. For example, failing to include demographic questions makes it impossible to later separate the responses by relevant groups. These points highlight the importance of planning and designing the survey. By the time you get to the analysis stage, it's too late to change anything.

The above facts often are overlooked when novices design surveys, so they may be news to you. Most likely basic statistics are not news to you, nor can they be described accurately as insider secrets. Nonetheless, this chapter addresses four basic types of data analysis to illustrate the point that they truly are sufficient for most types of business surveys. Below are descriptions of each one, along with examples of representative statistics. Not all types of analysis are appropriate or necessary for each survey.

Descriptive statistics describe various features of the data. They are useful for providing a quick look at the characteristics of your sample and the responses, as well as for determining whether there are any anomalies. For example:

- *Counts*: The number of times something occurs or is present in a data array.
- **n** represents the number of people in the sample or the number of responses. It is a subset of the population statistic (N). You should report the number and the percentage of usable responses to provide context.
- **Frequencies** indicate the number of times a given response is chosen. For example, on a 1-5 scale frequencies identify how many respondents chose #1, how many chose #2, etc. They also indicate where data are missing.

Measures of central tendency are single values that represent the center of a set of numerical observations. There are three primary measures:

- **Mean** is the average value of the data array.
- **Median** is the middle value of the data array and is used to reduce the impact of extreme values or outliers.
- **Mode** is the value that appears with the greatest frequency in the data array. Some data arrays have multiple modes.

Measures of variability or dispersion indicate how far from the mean the data fall. For example:

- *Range*: An indicator of how spread out the data are. It is defined by the minimum and maximum values in the data set (e.g., 1 to 5). Because it represents extreme values that may or may not be representative of the rest of the data, it has limited usefulness. However, as a descriptive statistic, it helps to identify errors or outliers relatively quickly.

- *Variance*: The average distance between each value and the mean. It indicates the extent to which the value differs from the typical value in the data array. For example, a high level of variance might indicate that respondents had sharply divergent answers to a given survey question.
- **Standard deviation**: A measure of how tightly or loosely data are clustered around the mean value. Standard deviation is the square root of the variance. A small value means data are tightly clustered around the mean and there is little variation; a high value means the data are dispersed.

Measures of relatedness indicate whether there is a relationship among variables and provide some information about the nature of the relationship. For example:

- *Correlation*: An indicator of the extent to which the value of two variables are related, if at all. If they are, the correlation coefficient shows whether the relationship is positive (the values move in the same direction) or negative (they move in opposite directions). Correlation does NOT indicate causation. All the correlation coefficient tells us is whether there is a relationship and its direction; it cannot tell us whether one variable causes the other.
- *Regression analysis*: A way of assessing causality among variables. A set of variables is tested to see which ones, if any, can predict the value of the designated outcome.

If your situation calls for more complex types of analysis than those described above, you would be well advised to hire an expert. In either case, after analyzing the data it's time to move to the final stage: reporting results and taking action.

Part 5:

Reporting Results and Taking Action

Chapter 22: Reporting Results

Insider Tip: Tell audiences only what they need to know.

After you have conducted the survey, analyzed the results, drawn the conclusions, and identified some recommendations, you still have two important steps to take: reporting the results and taking action. Here are nine issues relevant to reporting the results.

1. You must be honest in providing feedback, even when you know the audience doesn't want to hear it. Your credibility depends on your honesty.

2. The amount of information and level of detail will vary by constituent group. For example, the report sent to interested respondents (if promised) will summarize the highlights, whereas the report to executives will include much more detail. Be sure the information is in a format that is easily understandable and immediately useful to its intended audience.

3. If you promised respondents a summary of the results, provide it in a timely manner. Make sure the content has been approved by the decision makers.

4. The report should be narrowly focused on information that addresses the survey's purpose. Tell the audiences only what they need to know, not everything you know. Being succinct and direct is particularly challenging with qualitative data: you must resist the strong urge to let others know how much information you collected even when it's not directly relevant to the purpose of the study. Failure to resist that impulse will decrease the effectiveness of the survey because the results will be difficult to find.

5. Here is a suggested format for the report to executives:

    *   Purpose
    *   Description of the sample
    *   Description of survey method
    *   Findings
    *   Conclusions
    *   Recommendations for action

    The report also should include a one-page executive summary. Keep in mind that the summary is the only part of the report that some people will read, so make it count. For example, be sure it includes the conclusions as well as the recommendations for action.

6. Provide charts, tables and graphics only when they reinforce the narrative, or do a better job of making a point. Not every result needs to be shown in graphic form! Be sure to label the visuals clearly (e.g., in a font size that adults can read easily) and provide a key that explains their parts. Specify the unit of measurement (number, percent, etc.) even if it seems obvious to you.

7. Provide context for your findings so audiences can understand their importance easily and quickly. For example, reporting the **number** of employees who intend to leave the organization in the coming year has little meaning. However, reporting the **percentage** of employees who intend to leave allows decision makers to evaluate the importance of this fact. Reporting the percentage of **good performers** who intend to leave the organization is even more useful.

8. Provide results by sub-groups (work location, tenure with the organization, etc.) only when there are meaningful results. If analyses show no differences, you don't need to belabor that point graphically or in words.

9. Since people have different learning style preferences (reading, hearing, seeing, etc.), try to present the results in multiple formats so you are more likely to reach everyone effectively. For example, a written report with visual aids that is presented verbally covers three different learning styles.

The format of the report should be consistent with the survey's purpose. You don't need a thesis-length document to report what customer or employee preferences are for a new service, for example. Instead, provide only the information that is pertinent to the audience.

Chapter 23: Taking Action

Insider Tip: You are better off not conducting a survey at all than doing it and not taking action.

Taking action means organizational leaders do something to address the survey findings, whether they are good, bad, or indifferent. It does not mean they have to do everything that employees or customers ask them to do. At a minimum, they must respond to the findings. Saying "no" or "not now" to some of the recommendations is perfectly acceptable as long as you give a reason why. Doing nothing is unacceptable.

Extracting a commitment from leaders upfront to take action is critical to an effective survey process. Survey participants, especially those in low-trust environments, will be watching carefully to see what leaders do with the information they provided. Few things kill management credibility faster than a refusal to act on survey results. Participants become cynical, and you will likely notice negative consequences in the workplace such as lower productivity or poor morale.

For these reasons, it is important during the planning stage to ask leaders what they intend to do with the survey results, and what actions they are both willing and able to take. For example, if pay and benefits are completely off the table for change, the survey should not address these issues. If you're not willing or able to take any action, why conduct the survey?

Here are examples of actions that three different organizations took in response to findings from employee climate surveys:

1. A large health care organization whose skilled information technology employees were leaving in droves used the results of its employee survey to develop a retention plan that sharply decreased its 24% turnover rate. Most of the actions (e.g., recognition programs and adjusting processes to allow more employee input) cost little or nothing to implement. In fact, the majority of the recommendations were about reinstating things the organization used to do but dropped because they didn't think employees cared about them (e.g., celebrating achievement of project goals).

2. A small national defense contractor that found its highly trained junior analysts leaving after only three years, used the results of its employee climate survey to pinpoint the sources of dissatisfaction and make the changes necessary to address them. For example, existing information about career paths was made widely accessible instead of remaining "hidden" in notebooks on their managers' book shelves.

3. A large transportation company conducts an organization-wide employee survey each year. Results are communicated to managers who then conduct meetings with their staff to share the feedback and plan the relevant action. Upper management pay close attention to the reports that detail managers' results. The company uses its performance management system to hold managers accountable for taking appropriate action and making year-to-year improvements.

Asking employees or customers to take their time to answer survey questions is only the first step in making them feel they are being heard. The second critical step is taking appropriate actions based on their feedback. It's okay not to fix everything right now; you do not have to say "yes" to everything respondents want. Saying "no" or "not now" is fine as long as leaders explain their reasons for those answers. The reasons can be general rather than specific when necessary, as long as they are honest.

Chapter 24: Closing the Loop

> Insider Tip: The survey process is not over until you have evaluated what changes were made and whether they addressed the initial purpose.

One of the biggest mistakes organizations make when conducting surveys is assuming that the survey process is over once the results have been reported. In fact, there is one more step: determining whether the survey accomplished its stated purpose. Answering that question involves identifying the changes that were made as a result of the survey and evaluating their impact on the organization. What's different now than before the survey? Unless this follow-up is completed, you cannot truly determine the effectiveness of the survey process.

In order to conduct this type of assessment, the critical success factors identified in Chapter 1 must have been present from the start. You must have articulated a clear purpose, and identified measures that allow you to determine whether you achieved it. Your executive champions must have translated results to action and held people accountable for change. In short, you must have planned for this last step.

After the assessment, there is one last question: How will you maintain the momentum created by the survey process? Here are three suggestions to help you continue moving forward:

1. Provide quarterly updates on the changes, including the impact on the organization.

2. Tie the achievement of results to management performance evaluation.

3. Communicate the changes and link them specifically to employee or customer feedback so people know their voices were heard.

For those who feel ready to undertake their own survey process, congratulations! This booklet will serve as a handy guide for obtaining accurate, actionable information that will allow you to make any changes necessary to enhance your organization's success.

For those who would prefer to hire an expert for all or part of the process, the information in this booklet will help guide you in identifying those who fit your particular needs.

For those who have questions or comments, please let us hear from you!

Pat Lynch, Ph.D.
President
Business Alignment Strategies, Inc.

Pat Lynch is a consultant, coach, and speaker who helps successful executives and business owners optimize their business results by aligning people, programs, and processes with organizational goals. She is President of Business Alignment Strategies, Inc., a management consulting company in Long Beach, California.

A former university professor, Pat earned her Ph.D. in personnel and employment relations (human resources, labor relations, organizational behavior), with a minor in employment law, following a career in the Finance and Treasury divisions of FedEx Corporation. Prior to that, she held positions including manager, social worker, and credit analyst. She also served as an arbitrator for the New York Stock Exchange. Her survey expertise, initially grounded in her graduate studies, was refined considerably through her work with recognized experts during her doctoral program, and has been refined over the years by assisting her own clients with their employee and customer survey needs.

Pat is one of fewer than three dozen people worldwide who have been inducted into Alan Weiss's Million Dollar Consultant® Hall of Fame. She was recognized as being a human performance and productivity expert who has worked with highly effective results in public sector and other highly politicized environments.

One little-known fact about Pat is that as of 2010 she has walked eight marathons and over a dozen half-marathons to raise money and awareness for the Leukemia & Lymphoma Society.

To learn more about Pat, please contact her by phone or e-mail, or visit her on-line:

Pat Lynch, Ph.D.

Business Alignment >>>
STRATEGIES, INC.

Long Beach, CA 90815
Phone: (562) 985-0333
E-mail: Info@BusinessAlignmentStrategies.com
Web: www.BusinessAlignmentStrategies.com
Blog: www.OptimizeBusinessResults.com

www.ingramcontent.com/pod-product-compliance
Lightning Source LLC
Chambersburg PA
CBHW041215270326
41930CB00001B/22